NASA SPACE VEHICLES

Capsules, Shuttles, and Space Stations

Michael D. Cole

Series Advisor:
John E. McLeaish
Chief, Public Information Office, retired,
NASA Johnson Space Center

Enslow Publishers, Inc.

40 Industrial Road	PO Box 38
Box 398	Aldershot
Berkeley Heights, NJ 07922	Hants GU12 6BP
USA	UK

http://www.enslow.com

Library of Congress Cataloging-in-Publication Data

Cole, Michael D.
    NASA space vehicles : capsules, shuttles, and space stations / Michael D. Cole.
        p. cm. — (Countdown to space)
    Includes bibliographical references and index.
    Summary: Describes American space vehicles and their uses, including various space probes, the Mercury, Gemini, and Apollo capsules, Skylab, the space shuttles, and the International Space Station.
    ISBN 0-7660-1308-1
    1. Space vehicles—United States—History Juvenile literature. [1. Space vehicles. 2. Outer space—Exploration.] I. Title. II. Series.
    TL793.C6473   2000
    629.44'0973—dc21   99-35533
                                                                  CIP

Printed in the United States of America

10 9 8 7 6 5 4 3 2 1

To Our Readers: All Internet addresses in this book were active and appropriate when we went to press. Any comments or suggestions can be sent by e-mail to Comments@enslow.com or to the address on the back cover.

CONTENTS

The space shuttle Columbia, shown on the right, is only one of NASA's many space vehicles.

1

Vehicles and Humans in Space

The day was April 14, 1981. The space shuttle *Columbia* was coming to the end of its first mission in space. Thousands of heat tiles covered the new spacecraft. The tiles on the shuttle's underbelly glowed red-hot as *Columbia* began reentering Earth's atmosphere. *Columbia* was traveling very fast. At the spacecraft's high speed, friction with the atmosphere caused heat to build up on the surface of the tiles. If the tiles were not successful at protecting *Columbia* from the high heat of reentry, the spacecraft and the astronauts inside it would be burned up.

The space shuttle had never reentered Earth's atmosphere before. The heat tiles had been tested in furnaces, and against fiery blowtorches on Earth. But no one knew if the tiles would really work in space. Some of the tiles at the rear of the shuttle had already come off during the launch. Everyone working on the mission hoped that the reentry would be successful, especially the shuttle's astronauts, John Young and Robert Crippen.

"We're showing about eighty-five miles," Young said, telling Mission Control about the shuttle's altitude above Earth.

"Roger," the capsule communicator, or capcom, replied from Mission Control. "Moving right along. Nice and easy does it, John. We're all riding with you."[1]

Minutes earlier the shuttle had been traveling at its

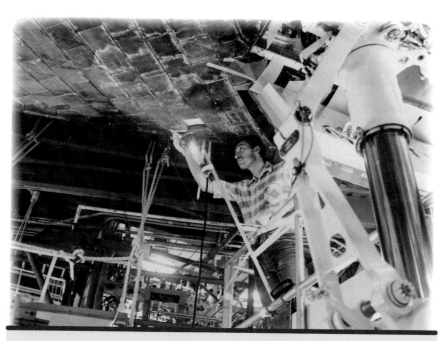

A technician repairs the space shuttle's tiles. The tiles are used for heat protection during reentry into Earth's atmosphere.

orbital speed of 17,500 miles per hour. Rockets had been fired to slow the spacecraft so that it would begin its fall toward Earth. Now, friction with the atmosphere was causing the spacecraft to rapidly slow down. That same friction with the atmosphere created the intense heat on the outside of the shuttle. The temperature on the outside of *Columbia* soon climbed to more than 2,750°F, a temperature hot enough to melt gold or silver.

The high temperature created a barrier of heated molecules around the shuttle that no radio signal could penetrate. Young and Crippen could not communicate with Mission Control for fifteen minutes. As NASA and a large television audience around the United States waited to see if the heat tiles would work, there was silence.

Finally, Young's voice came through loud and clear: "Hello, Houston. *Columbia* here," he said.[2]

The tiles had worked, shielding *Columbia* successfully through reentry. By now the shuttle had slowed down to about five thousand miles per hour. At this speed, the shuttle's wings allowed it to glide through the air. John Young took over the controls of *Columbia*.

Young was about to make *Columbia* do what no other American space vehicle had ever done before. All previous American spacecraft had floated on parachutes to a splashdown in the ocean. Young was going to bring the space shuttle down like an airplane, gliding it to a rolling touchdown on land.

Within minutes, *Columbia* was gliding toward the

wide salt flats near Edwards Air Force Base in California. Because the shuttle was gliding without any power of its own, Young would not be able to circle the shuttle around again. He had only one chance to get the landing right. If he made a mistake, they would crash.

The landing gear unfolded from the bottom of the shuttle. Young gently set the back two wheels down. Then, very slowly, the shuttle's nose came down, and

John Young (left) and Robert Crippen give a "thumbs up" signal from the flight deck of the Columbia shuttle. Young had only one chance to land the shuttle correctly. If he made a mistake, the shuttle would crash.

The pilot has only one chance to land the shuttle. The parachute opens to help the vehicle glide to a stop.

the nose wheels touched the ground. The shuttle then coasted along the landing area for almost a mile until it stopped.[3]

Columbia—the world's first space vehicle to return from space and land like an airplane—was home!

"This is the world's greatest flying machine, I'll tell you that," Young said as the shuttle came to a stop. "It worked super."[4]

The space shuttle, the world's first reusable manned space vehicle, is one of the most complex machines ever built. But the space shuttle is only the latest vehicle in which astronauts have traveled into space.

Humans began their exploration of space in 1961. Since then, they have traveled in a number of different space vehicles.

2

From Mercury to Gemini

The first American space vehicles were very different from the spacecraft used today. They were designed to carry only one person into space, and they were not reusable. The spacecraft made only one flight. A new spacecraft was built for the next mission.

American astronauts completed their first space missions in the Mercury spacecraft. The Mercury spacecraft was a very small cone-shaped vehicle. The astronauts stayed inside the spacecraft, sometimes called a capsule, until it floated on parachutes and splashed down in the ocean.

The first American astronaut in space, Alan Shepard, flew in a Mercury capsule, *Freedom 7*. The astronauts selected to fly the Mercury spacecraft could not be taller than five feet ten inches, because of the spacecraft's limited cockpit space. For this reason, a Mercury astronaut was labeled as a *man in a can*.[1] The capsule was nine and a half feet long and weighed about four thousand pounds. It was about the size of a small car.[2] Shepard had to slither very carefully into *Freedom 7*'s cramped cockpit. The capsule lifted off from Cape Canaveral on May 5, 1961.

The Mercury capsule had a porthole, a periscope, and a system of thrusters that could change the spacecraft's position in space. A small instrument showed the spacecraft's position above Earth. A communication system kept Shepard in touch with Mercury Control, and a life support system supplied him with oxygen.[3]

Shepard and *Freedom 7* were rocketed into space for a suborbital flight. The capsule did not orbit, or go around, Earth. Instead, Shepard and his Mercury

Astronaut Alan Shepard was cramped inside his Mercury capsule.

capsule went into space and came back down on a flight lasting only fifteen minutes.

A retro-rocket pack was attached to the wider end of the cone-shaped capsule. The rocket pack, about the size of a large truck tire, was held against the capsule's heat shield by a set of metal straps. After the retro-rocket pack fired to slow the capsule down, the pack was cut loose from the capsule. The heat shield was left exposed to face the heat of reentry. This broad and protected end of the spacecraft was then turned toward Earth to begin reentry.

Shepard and the other astronauts kept their Mercury spacecraft at the proper angle during reentry so that the heat-shield surface could protect the capsule and themselves from burning up in the high heat.

Following reentry, parachutes sprung from the nose of the capsule. Shepard and

This small cone-shaped Mercury capsule is being lifted to the top of a rocket. The retro-rocket pack is attached to the bottom of the capsule.

Freedom 7 drifted safely to a splashdown in the Atlantic Ocean.

Two months later, astronaut Gus Grissom completed a similar flight. In February 1962, John Glenn made the first orbital flight in a Mercury spacecraft. There were six Mercury flights in all, ending with Gordon Cooper's twenty-two-orbit flight in 1963.

The next American spacecraft was very similar to Mercury. It was a larger and improved version of the earlier craft, redesigned to carry more than one space

A workman cleans a Mercury heat shield. Without its protection, the capsule and the astronaut inside would burn up during reentry.

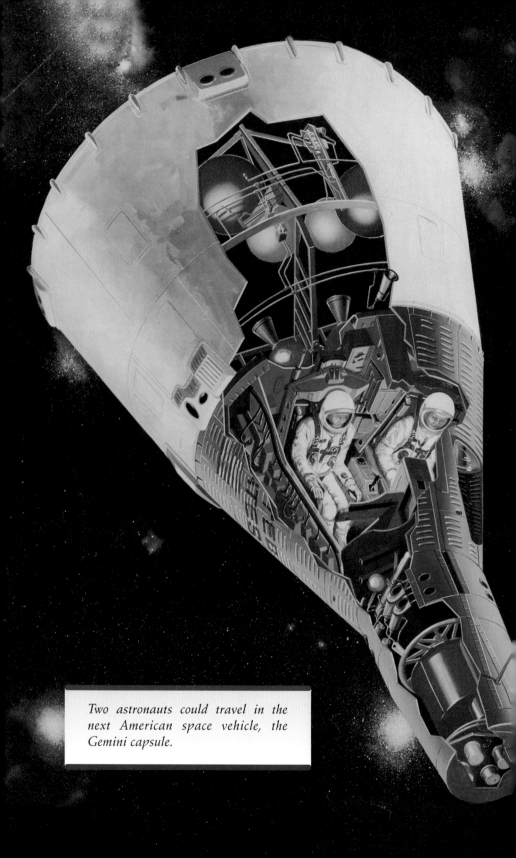

Two astronauts could travel in the next American space vehicle, the Gemini capsule.

traveler. This new two-person spacecraft was named Gemini. The name comes from the Latin word meaning "twins." Attached to the rear of the capsule was a maneuvering system that could change the orbit of the spacecraft. The nose was redesigned so that it could dock, or become linked, with another vehicle in space. The capsule's hatches were hinged so that astronauts could leave the spacecraft for spacewalks.

There were no air locks on Gemini. When it was time to do a spacewalk, both astronauts pressurized their space suits against the deadly environment of space. Then they simply opened the hatch and allowed the capsule's cabin to be depressurized. One astronaut did the spacewalk while the other remained in the cabin.

When the spacewalk was over, the hatch was pulled shut, sealed, and the cabin repressurized. Edward White became the first American to walk in space when he floated gently out from the hatch of *Gemini 4* in June 1965.

There were ten Gemini flights. These missions tested the abilities of both the astronauts and the spacecraft to change orbit, dock in space, and work outside the capsule in a space suit. The Gemini spacecraft and its ten space missions gave NASA much valuable information and experience in the complex operation of spaceflight.

It was all preparation for the next space vehicle that would carry astronauts to the Moon.

3

Space Vehicles
to the Moon

Project Apollo was NASA's program to send astronauts to the Moon. It used two very different spacecraft to accomplish its historic goal.

The command and service module (CSM) was made up of a cone-shaped command module that was attached to a cylindrical service module. The command module, or crew capsule, held the three astronauts and their equipment. The service module contained the engine, fuel cells, and other power systems for the spacecraft. Connected to the CSM was the lunar module (LM). The LM was a spiderlike vehicle with four landing legs. Once in orbit around the Moon, the LM could detach from the CSM to descend and make a landing on the lunar surface.

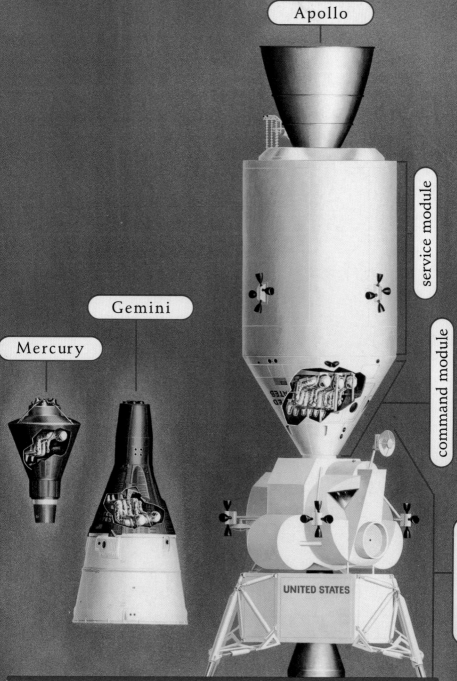

Apollo

service module

Gemini

command module

Mercury

lunar module

UNITED STATES

This illustration compares the Mercury, Gemini, and Apollo capsules. The Apollo vehicle's command module is attached to the service module and the lunar module.

The two spacecraft were launched into space on top of a gigantic Saturn V rocket. The Saturn V was the most powerful machine ever built at that time. It produced 7.5 million pounds of thrust. The Saturn V needed all of this power to get the two Apollo spacecraft into orbit, then shoot them away from Earth toward the Moon.[1]

Four Apollo missions tested the rocket and the two spacecraft in space. These missions were in preparation for the first mission to land on the Moon—*Apollo 11*. Each Apollo crew was made up of three astronauts. The crew members for *Apollo 11* were commander Neil Armstrong, lunar module pilot Edwin "Buzz" Aldrin, and command module pilot Michael Collins.

Apollo 11 lifted off from Cape Canaveral on July 16, 1969. The Saturn V rocket made a thunderous roar as it rumbled off the launchpad to begin its historic journey. After burning all its fuel, the first stage of the Saturn V rocket dropped away. The second-stage rocket immediately fired, carrying the astronauts and their two space vehicles the rest of the way into orbit. After a few orbits, the third-stage rocket fired to push the spacecraft out of Earth's orbit, putting it on a course toward the Moon.

A short time after leaving Earth's orbit, the CSM separated from the third-stage rocket. Moving a short distance ahead, the CSM then turned around to dock with the LM, which was still housed inside the third-stage rocket. Collins used the CSM's maneuvering rockets to pull the LM out of the third-stage rocket housing. Docked nose to nose, the two spacecraft continued their 240,000-mile journey toward the Moon.

It took about two days for the Apollo spacecraft to reach the Moon. When the three *Apollo 11* astronauts arrived in orbit around the Moon, Armstrong and Aldrin crawled into the lunar module to begin preparing the spacecraft for its lunar landing. As soon as all systems aboard the LM were ready, the LM separated from the CSM. Michael Collins remained inside the command module, which continued to orbit the Moon.

Shortly after the LM separated from the CSM,

The command and service module (right) is docked to the lunar module (LM) on the left. The astronauts could crawl into the LM and land it on the Moon.

Armstrong and Aldrin began guiding the LM down toward the lunar surface with the aid of onboard computers. Inside the LM, the cockpit was very cramped. The spacecraft had no seats. Armstrong and Aldrin stood in front of their instruments, Armstrong to the left, Aldrin to the right. A pair of triangle-shaped windows were just above each of their instrument stations. Armstrong watched the Moon's landscape passing by while Aldrin gave him readings from the flight instruments.[2]

As the LM came closer to the surface, Armstrong saw that the area where the spacecraft was about to land was scattered with boulders. He quickly took manual control. Armstrong used the LM's hand controls to guide the spacecraft over the boulders toward a safer landing area. After some tense moments, the LM's landing legs finally touched down on the lunar surface with only seconds of fuel to spare.[3]

Hours after the lunar module landed, the astronauts got into their space suits and crawled out backward through a hatch in the front of the spacecraft.

Armstrong: How am I doing?

Aldrin: You're doing fine.

Armstrong: Okay. Houston, I'm on the porch.

Mission Control: Roger, Neil.[4]

Then they stepped down a ladder on one of the LM's landing legs and onto the Moon. When Armstrong stepped onto the Moon he said, "That's one small step for a man; one giant leap for mankind."[5] Once on the surface, the astronauts set up scientific equipment, conducted experiments, and collected samples of Moon rocks.

When the astronauts finished their work on the Moon, they crawled back into the LM. The part of the LM the astronauts rode in was called the ascent stage. This was the spiderlike upper part of the spacecraft. The ascent stage had its own rocket engine called the ascent engine, which would blast the ascent stage off the lunar surface and back into orbit around the Moon. The lower part of the LM was the descent stage. Its descent engine and landing legs had landed the LM safely on the lunar surface.

After storing their Moon rocks and equipment, the astronauts prepared to lift off from the Moon. They flipped switches that detached the ascent stage from the descent stage. At the end of the countdown, the LM's ascent stage lifted off from the Moon, leaving the descent stage with its spent engine and landing legs behind on the lunar surface.

The spiderlike lunar landing vehicle carried astronauts to the Moon.

The astronauts in the LM returned to lunar orbit and soon redocked with the CSM. On *Apollo 11*, command module pilot Collins was glad to see Armstrong and Aldrin emerge through the tunnel with their precious cargo of Moon rocks. The two boxes of rocks were carried from the lunar module and put into storage containers on the command module.[6]

The LM's job was now done. When the hatch that had connected the two spacecraft was sealed, the LM's ascent stage was cast away into space. The empty spacecraft eventually crashed onto the surface of the Moon. Only the CSM remained.

The CSM's engines then fired to put the spacecraft on a course back to Earth. Two and a half days later, the three astronauts in the CSM arrived back in Earth's atmosphere. The command module containing the astronauts and Moon rocks separated from the service module, which was left to float in space. The command module pilot maneuvered the capsule around until its heat shield faced the proper angle toward Earth. The heat shield glowed red during reentry through Earth's atmosphere. Soon after reentry, parachutes sprung from the nose of the command module, and the Apollo spacecraft drifted to a splashdown in the ocean.

Six Apollo missions landed on the Moon. *Apollo 13* did not land. The crew of *Apollo 13* barely made it back to Earth alive after an explosion aboard the CSM crippled their spacecraft. The Apollo Moon-landing program ended in 1972.

The last flight of an Apollo spacecraft came in 1975, when an Apollo CSM docked with a Russian Soyuz spacecraft in the *Apollo-Soyuz* mission. On this flight, American astronauts and Russian cosmonauts met and conducted experiments together in space. The *Apollo-Soyuz* mission was the first time the United States and Russia worked together in a space operation.

The Apollo capsules were recovered after they splashed down in the ocean.

For the next six years, no American astronauts flew into space. They were waiting for a new space vehicle to be developed. The new space vehicle would not drop away all of its rockets to never be used again. It would not float back to Earth on parachutes to splashdown in the ocean. Instead, the spacecraft would take off like a rocket, and land on the ground like an airplane. It is called the space shuttle.

4

Space Shuttles

On April 12, 1981, the first space shuttle, *Columbia*, lifted off from Cape Canaveral. *Columbia* was the world's first reusable spacecraft.

Columbia, Discovery, Atlantis, and *Challenger* were the first four space shuttles. *Challenger* exploded shortly after liftoff in January 1986, killing all seven crew members. It was later replaced by *Endeavour*, bringing the number of shuttles back up to four.

NASA uses these space shuttles as their reusable manned spacecraft. The program of moving the four space shuttles through the cycle of launch, landing, and preparation for the next mission is called the Space Transportation System, or STS. Each shuttle mission is given an STS number. For example, the flight of the space shuttle *Discovery* on which astronaut John Glenn became the oldest human ever to fly in space was called STS-95.

The space shuttle launch assembly consists of four parts: the orbiter, the large orange external tank, and two solid rocket boosters (SRBs).

The space shuttle orbiter is the spacecraft that carries the astronaut crew and their equipment into space. It is attached directly to the external tank during launch. The orbiter is about the size of a standard commercial passenger jet, but its shape is very different. Unlike most commercial jets, with wings protruding outward from an area somewhere near the middle of the aircraft, the space shuttle orbiter is a delta-winged craft. The wings begin near the front of the spacecraft and sweep back at an angle all the way to the rear of the vehicle. Such a design gives the spacecraft a triangular, or delta, shape when viewed from overhead.

The orbiter also has rocket engines. At T minus six seconds in the countdown, the engines start, to help launch the spacecraft into orbit.

The external tank is the largest component of the launch assembly. It is a 154-foot-tall insulated tank that carries all of the shuttle's liquid fuel for liftoff. The orbiter's three main rocket engines carry no fuel of their own. All of their fuel—1.5 million pounds of liquid hydrogen and liquid oxygen—is pumped from the external tank at a rate of 1,000 gallons per second.[1]

The external tank is the only part of the launch assembly that is not reusable. Once the shuttle reaches orbit, the external tank separates and is broken up in the atmosphere.

The solid rocket boosters (SRBs) are attached to either side of the external tank. These two 149-foot-tall boosters contain solid propellants, which are like explosive powders. When the countdown reaches zero, the SRBs ignite, helping the main engines lift the shuttle off the pad and accelerate it to a speed of more than 2,800 miles per hour. Two minutes and four seconds after the launch, the SRBs fall away from the external tank and the orbiter. They float down by parachute to the Atlantic Ocean, where they are later recovered for reuse on another launch. The orbiter and external

The shuttle launch assembly consists of the winged orbiter, the external tank, and two solid rocket boosters (SRBs). The SRBs are attached to each side of the orange external tank.

The UTC Liberty *tows a solid rocket booster that has splashed down in the ocean.*

tank continue accelerating toward space for the next six and a half minutes.[2]

Eight and a half minutes after launch, the shuttle's main engines shut down and the external tank separates from the orbiter. The astronauts and their spacecraft orbit 70 miles above Earth, traveling at a speed of 17,500 miles per hour.

But the launch sequence is not completely over. About forty-five minutes after launch, the shuttle pilot activates two rocket thrusters on the rear of the spacecraft. These smaller rocket thrusters are located near the orbiter's main engines. They are called the orbital maneuvering system, or OMS, engines. The shuttle pilot performs one burn of the OMS engines. This burn makes the orbit more circular, and raises the shuttle's orbit to an altitude of about one hundred fifty miles above Earth.[3]

When in orbit, the astronauts can take off the helmets and space suits that they wore during launch. It is comfortable enough inside the cabin for the astronauts to work in pants and short-sleeve shirts.

The shuttle's crew cabin is at the front of the orbiter. The upper deck of the crew cabin is the flight deck. All flight control instruments are on this deck, and the shuttle's commander and pilot fly the shuttle from the cockpit seats nearest the cabin's windows. At the rear of the flight deck are two windows that look out into the shuttle's payload bay. The payload bay is the largest part of the shuttle. It is the long, empty area where large objects such as satellites are placed to be carried into space aboard the shuttle.

Upon reaching orbit astronauts open the shuttle's payload bay doors. They open wide, exposing the interior of the payload bay to space. The insides of the payload bay doors are lined with a special radiating system. This important lining allows the heat created by the shuttle's electrical and life-support systems to be radiated away from the orbiter into space. Without this system, the interior of the shuttle would overheat.[4]

Below the windows at the rear of the flight deck are the controls for the remote manipulator system (RMS). The RMS is a robotic arm attached to the inside of the payload bay. Looking out the rear windows of the flight

Astronaut Scott Parazynski handles a joystick with his right hand to control the space shuttle's robotic arm. The window in front of him overlooks the payload bay.

deck, astronauts at the RMS controls use the robotic arm to help move objects in and out of the payload bay. The RMS has been used many times to help launch satellites, and snag satellites out of orbit for repair. It was also a big help to astronauts during the complex repair missions on the Hubble Space Telescope.[5]

The lower deck of the shuttle's crew cabin is called the mid-deck. It is an area that serves many purposes. Astronauts not only conduct experiments in this area, but also eat, sleep, exercise, and go to the bathroom here.

The forward wall of the mid-deck is lined with several compartments that contain the food and drinks

The doors of the shuttle's payload bay are opened wide when orbit is reached.

the astronauts will consume during their mission. Other compartments contain equipment for experiments and the personal belongings of the astronauts. A treadmill is attached to the floor. It has a harness that holds the astronauts to the treadmill so that they may get some exercise in zero gravity. Crew members sleep in sleep restraints, which are like sleeping bags clipped to the wall, to prevent the sleeping astronaut from floating around the cabin. Astronauts go to the bathroom in the personal hygiene station.

During the shuttle's launch, three temporary seats are firmly attached to the floor of the mid-deck. Three crew members sit in these seats until after the shuttle reaches orbit. The seats are folded and stowed during the rest of the mission. The shuttle's commander, pilot, and two other astronauts are strapped into seats on the flight deck.

At the rear of the mid-deck is the hatch that astronauts use to enter the payload bay. When astronauts conduct a spacewalk during their mission, this hatch provides their way to the outside. This hatch is the spacewalking astronauts' doorway into space.

Conducting a series of experiments during the flight is often the main focus of a shuttle mission. When this is the case, the orbiter's payload bay is occupied by a spacelab module. The module gives the astronauts more room to perform in-orbit experiments, and contains the equipment, supplies, and tools they need to conduct the

Two astronauts used the round open hatch to enter the payload bay and perform their spacewalks.

experiments. The spacelab module is sealed directly to the mid-deck hatchway. Astronauts can then move easily between the mid-deck area and the spacelab module.

Space shuttle missions usually last between five and fourteen days. Near the completion of the mission, all materials and equipment are stored. The seats are unfolded and clamped back in the same positions they were in during launch. Crew members again put on their space suits and helmets. The payload bay doors are slowly closed. The commander and pilot turn the shuttle so that the OMS engines can be fired to slow the shuttle's velocity. Within minutes, the spacecraft is no longer traveling fast enough to remain in orbit. It begins its arcing descent toward Earth.

The heat tiles on the belly of the shuttle begin to glow as it reenters Earth's atmosphere. Radio contact between the shuttle and Mission Control is lost for about fifteen minutes. The shuttle emerges from that period and reestablishes radio contact. The commander and pilot now take control of the shuttle's flight. With no power of its own, the shuttle must glide the rest of the way toward its landing. The commander must land it like an airplane. The landing site for most shuttle missions is the three-mile-long landing strip at Kennedy Space Center in Florida. Bad weather in Florida at the conclusion of a mission sometimes forces mission planners to have the shuttle land at Edwards Air Force Base in California.

The shuttle comes in steep toward the runway, at twice the speed of a commercial airliner. Upon landing, another successful mission is completed.[6] Hours after the crew exits the orbiter and the spacecraft is powered down, the process of preparing the shuttle for another flight begins. Experimental materials and other equipment used during the mission are removed from the orbiter. By the following day, the shuttle is already into the first phase of its inspection. Every part of the spacecraft will be fully inspected to prepare it for its next mission into space.

As the twenty-first century begins, the space shuttle is a very busy vehicle. It has a very important role in building the International Space Station.

5

Space Stations, Space Probes, and Beyond

America launched its first space station in 1973. *Skylab* was a small space station, about the size of a large house trailer. Two solar arrays were attached to its sides. This made it look like a large windmill.[1] It was designed to conduct experiments in space and test the long-term endurance of astronauts in the space environment. Three crews of three astronauts were sent to *Skylab*. Apollo CSMs were used to carry the crews to and from the space station. This successful space station dropped out of orbit on July 11, 1979.

The International Space Station (ISS) is a larger and far more complex space station than NASA's *Skylab*. It is a space vehicle like no other.

The Skylab space vehicle was America's first manned station in space.

The modules of the International Space Station were designed and constructed by a number of different space agencies around the world. The first crew is scheduled to occupy the station in 2000. At least twenty-seven space shuttle flights and forty-four Russian rocket launches will be required to complete construction on the station.[2]

When construction is completed, the orbiting ISS will equal the length of three football fields. The station will be able to hold a crew of six. These crew members will live in habitation modules and work in the station's various laboratories. A larger remote manipulator system, similar to the robotic arm on the space shuttle, will aid in repairing and servicing satellites and other spacecraft brought to the station.

The ISS is designed to serve as an orbital outpost. It will provide a permanent facility in which to conduct scientific research in the weightless environment of space.

While scientists and engineers use the station and

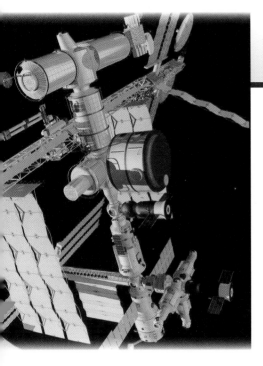

The International Space Station (ISS) is larger than Skylab. *The ISS is a permanent laboratory in space.*

the space shuttle to learn more about how humans can live and work in space, other space vehicles have been exploring the solar system and beyond. Since the 1960s, many robotic spacecraft have journeyed far into space. These vehicles are helping to prepare the way for further human exploration.

Two of the most important vehicles NASA has sent to explore the solar system are *Voyager 1* and *Voyager 2*. Both vehicles were launched in 1977, and arrived at Jupiter four months apart in 1979. The two spacecraft transmitted the first detailed images of the giant planet, including its four major moons. Both *Voyager 1* and *Voyager 2* then moved on to Saturn, where they took the first close-up pictures of Saturn's complex system of rings. The spacecraft studied the planet's thick atmosphere and sent back images of Saturn's many moons, which the spacecraft discovered totaled more than twenty.[3]

Voyager 1 headed out of the solar system, while

Voyager 2's mission was altered to continue to Uranus and Neptune. *Voyager 2* flew by Uranus in 1986, and completed its study of Neptune in 1989 before heading into interstellar space.

A far more detailed study of Jupiter was accomplished by the *Galileo* spacecraft starting in 1995. *Galileo* orbited Jupiter, collecting data about the planet's atmosphere, its huge rotating storm called the Great Red Spot, and the properties of its four major moons. The *Galileo* spacecraft included an atmospheric probe that separated and descended into Jupiter's atmosphere. *Galileo* recorded the information from the probe and sent it back to Earth.

Some robotic space vehicles have landed on other planets. In November 1996, the Mars Global Surveyor was launched to study the Red Planet. The goal of this mission is to map the surface of Mars. On July 4, 1997, *Pathfinder* landed on Mars and released the robotic rover called *Sojourner*. The rover moved slowly around the rocky rust-colored surface of Mars. It took many pictures and gathered important information about Martian soil and rocks.

The Hubble Space Telescope is a truly unique spacecraft that has allowed astronomers to see nearly to the edge of the universe. Throughout the 1990s, it recorded sharp, clear images of planets, stars, nebulas, and distant galaxies. From its place in high Earth-orbit, Hubble transmits these images to the Space Telescope

The Hubble Space Telescope sits in the payload bay of the shuttle. Hubble allows astronomers to see sharp images of planets, stars, and distant galaxies.

Science Institute in Baltimore, Maryland, where teams of astronomers study them.

Before the middle of the twenty-first century, new space vehicles may carry human beings to Mars. Unmanned spacecraft will need to go ahead of them, landing a power-generating system on the planet, as well as supplies and equipment. Later, the day may come when the first astronauts land on Mars.

Their accomplishment would come after many decades of learning and experimenting in space. Since the late 1950s, it has taken the designing, building, testing, and flying of many space vehicles to get these first human beings to Mars. It may not end there. From this first landing on Mars, space exploration can continue.

Space vehicles, both manned and unmanned, are the key to our future in space. Whether they are sending information to Earth from a distant world, or carrying us to a landing on another planet, space vehicles play a very important part in our exploration and understanding of the universe.

CHAPTER NOTES

Chapter 1. Vehicles and Humans in Space

1. NASA, *First Flight of the Shuttle Columbia* (Houston, Tex.: Finley-Holiday Film Corp., 1981).

2. Ibid.

3. Peter Bond, *Heroes in Space: From Gagarin to Challenger* (New York: Basil Blackwell, 1987), p. 401.

4. NASA.

Chapter 2. From Mercury to Gemini

1. William E. Burrows, *This New Ocean: The Story of the First Space Age* (New York: Random House, Inc., 1998), p. 289.

2. Ibid., p. 288.

3. David Baker, *The History of Manned Space Flight* (New York: Crown Publishers, 1982), p. 75.

Chapter 3. Space Vehicles to the Moon

1. Valerie Neal, Cathleen Lewis, and Frank Winter, *Spaceflight: A Smithsonian Guide* (New York: Macmillan Company, 1995), p. 57.

2. Alan Shepard and Deke Slayton, *Moon Shot: The Inside Story of America's Race to the Moon* (Atlanta: Turner Publishing, 1994), p. 23.

3. Ibid., pp. 25–29.

4. Eric M. Jones, "One Small Step," *Apollo 11 Lunar Surface Journal*, May 2, 1999, <http://www.hq.nasa.gov/office/pao/History/alsj/frame.html> (June 14, 1999).

5. Ibid.

6. Michael Collins, *Liftoff: The Story of America's Adventure in Space* (New York: Grove Press, 1988), p. 10.

Chapter 4. Space Shuttles

1. Michael Collins, *Liftoff: The Story of America's Adventure in Space* (New York: Grove Press, 1988), p. 209.

2. Wayne Lee, *To Rise from Earth: An Easy-to-Understand Guide to Spaceflight* (New York: Facts On File, Inc., 1995), pp. 178–184.

3. Ibid., p. 186.

4. Ibid., p. 192.

5. *Rescue Mission in Space: The Hubble Space Telescope*, NOVA Adventures in Science video (1994).

6. Peter Bond, *Heroes in Space: From Gagarin to Challenger* (New York: Basil Blackwell, 1987), p. 401.

Chapter 5. Space Stations, Space Probes, and Beyond

1. William E. Burrows, *This New Ocean: The Story of the First Space Age* (New York: Random House, Inc., 1998), p. 444.

2. Wayne Lee, *To Rise from Earth: An Easy-to-Understand Guide to Spaceflight* (New York: Facts On File, Inc., 1995), p. 221.

3. Valerie Neal, Cathleen Lewis, and Frank Winter, *Spaceflight: A Smithsonian Guide* (New York: Macmillan Company, 1995), p. 178.

GLOSSARY

air lock—An airtight chamber separating areas of different air pressure. Astronauts in space suits move into an air-lock chamber, seal it, allow the chamber to equalize with the pressure of the area where they are going, and open the air-lock door in that direction.

altitude—The distance of an airplane, spacecraft, or any other object from the ground or sea level.

command and service module (CSM)—The Apollo spacecraft that carried astronauts to the Moon. The CSM remained in lunar orbit, while the lunar module (LM) landed on the Moon.

external tank—The large tank that carries all the liquid fuel for the space shuttle orbiter's main engines. After the shuttle reaches orbit, the tank separates from the orbiter and is broken up in Earth's atmosphere.

hatch—Doors on spacecraft that allow astronauts to move in and out of the spacecraft, or between separate pressurized compartments of a spacecraft. When closed, hatches are sealed to keep air pressure within the spacecraft.

heat shield—The surface on the blunt end of early spacecraft. Parts of the surface were designed to burn away to carry the heat away and prevent heat from building up on the spacecraft.

lunar module (LM)—The Apollo spacecraft that landed astronauts on the Moon.

nebula—A large cloud of gas and dust in space. A nebula may be the remains of a star that has exploded or may be the collapsing dust cloud of a "nursery" where new stars are being born.

reentry—The phase of a spaceflight in which astronauts and their spacecraft return home through Earth's atmosphere. The high velocity of their return through the atmosphere causes friction with air molecules. The friction produces intense heat on the outside of the spacecraft, requiring the spacecraft to be equipped with a heat shield.

retro-rockets—Spacecraft rockets that are fired to slow the spacecraft's velocity.

simulation—Any activity that allows astronauts to prepare and practice for the situations they will encounter in space. Their simulations use equipment that is identical to what they will use in space, and create an environment similar to the conditions they will experience in orbit.

solid rocket boosters (SRBs)—The two rockets attached to both sides of the space shuttle launch assembly's external tank. The SRBs burn explosive powders for the first two minutes of the launch before separating from the launch assembly. They fall to the ocean where they are later recovered.

thrusters—System of small rockets used to control the position of a spacecraft.

FURTHER READING

Books

Baird, Anne. *The U.S. Space Camp Book of Rockets*. New York: William Morrow and Co., Inc., 1994.

Bondar, Barbara, and Roberta Bondar. *On the Shuttle: Eight Days in Space*. Buffalo, N.Y.: Firefly Books Limited, 1995.

Cole, Michael D. *Apollo 11: First Moon Landing*. Springfield, N.J.: Enslow Publishers, Inc., 1995.

———. *Columbia: First Flight of the Space Shuttle*. Springfield, N.J.: Enslow Publishers, Inc., 1995.

———. *Galileo Spacecraft: Mission to Jupiter*. Springfield, N.J.: Enslow Publishers, Inc., 1999.

Lee, Wayne. *To Rise from Earth: An Easy-to-Understand Guide to Spaceflight*. New York: Facts On File, Inc., 1995.

Neal, Valerie, Cathleen Lewis, and Frank White. *Spaceflight: A Smithsonian Guide*. New York: Macmillan, 1995.

Shorto, Russell. *How to Fly the Space Shuttle*. Sante Fe, N.M.: John Muir Publications, 1992.

Snedden, Robert. *Rockets and Spacecraft*. Austin, Tex.: Raintree Steck-Vaughn Publishers, 1998.

Internet Addresses

Bulashova, Natasha, and Greg Cole. "Russian Space Vehicles." *Friends and Partners.* April 2, 1999. <http://www.friends-partners.org/oldfriends/jgreen/ ruvehicl.html> (November 12, 1998).

Evans, Mike, Steve Johnson, Joshua Cohen, David Lackner, and Joel Rademacher. *Mission and Spacecraft Library.* n.d. <http://msl.jpl.nasa.gov/> (November 10, 1998).

Fisher, Diane, Nancy Leon, and Dr. Marc Rayman. *The Space Place.* April 1, 1999. <http:// spaceplace.jpl.nasa.gov/> (November 20, 1998).

Kennedy Space Center Homepage. April 12, 1999. <http://www.ksc.nasa.gov> (November 15, 1998).

INDEX